The TEOTWAWKI Tuxedo

Formal Survival Attire

By Joe Nobody

Prepper Press

Publishing to Help You Prepare

www.PrepperPress.com

www.HoldingYourGround.com

The TEOTWAWKI Tuxedo Defensive Formal Attire

Introduction

The purpose of this book is to provide a reference guide for those who will be defending a property in a SHTF or TEOTWAWKI environment. Specifically, it addresses personal equipment such as clothing, medical kits, and bug-out bags from a defensive perspective.

There are hundreds of sources available for self-defense, and that is important as well. The *HOLDING* series of books is intended to provide guidance for defending, or security of, a location. Normally, for people who prepare, this is called a bug-out location or BOL.

Regardless of bugging in or out, you and your family will have to reside somewhere. There is a chance that you will have to defend it from looters, scavengers, or other types of predators.

Most people who start "preparing" for bad times quickly realize that it is practically impossible to address every scenario. There are too many options, too much expense, and too many unknowns. I have met home owners who have made an extensive investment in solar power systems, only to become frustrated when they read that an Electro Magnetic Pulse (EMP) event would probably disable the entire system.

While it is not productive to dwell on all the possible "What if?" scenarios, it may be prudent to consider what simple elementary and intermediate steps each of us can take to be in a position to protect our loved ones. Properly equipping yourself for defensive action is not expensive. Most of the items recommended in this book have dual purposes and can provide benefit even if the "event" never occurs.

An argument can be made that no other preparations are complete without security plans being in place. If the scenario involves looting or theft, no matter how much food you have stored, it won't do you any good if someone comes in and takes it all. While the *HOLDING* series of books addresses precautions and actions that can be executed for a physical location, you as a person will require some preparation as well. What clothing you wear, what "kit" you have available and how you manage your assets are all important and are addressed within.

Any "defense" is really just a "system" with various components that work together. Like any system, the weakest component will cause problems. It would not make any sense to have the best weapons without a way to carry ammunition. That system would fail.

Preparing, or being a "Prepper" as we sometimes refer to ourselves, is not a socially acceptable activity in many circles. Most people don't want their friends or neighbors knowing their beliefs or activities. Most of us consider ourselves "model" citizens and productive members of a society, so the concept of preparing for the decline of said society is not a natural act. Defensive planning and preparation can be performed in the privacy of your own home and with other individuals with whom you share similar beliefs.

Prologue

As I started researching this book, many people asked me the same basic question:

"Why write a book about such a simple topic?"

A few years ago, I would have agreed 100%. Who needs it? After all, millions of people pack up with a heavy load and go camping or hiking every year. Most of them accomplish this without reading a book. The same can be said of soldiers going off to war.

The following story will explain why I began writing this book:

A few years ago I was driving home on a Friday afternoon suffering from a very stressful week. Business deadlines, fighting between co-workers and lots of other things were weighing on my mind. It had been the worst week I could remember, and I knew I was going to be an unpleasant person over the weekend.

I craved to be outdoors. I needed to feel grass and dirt under my boots and smell a camp fire. I needed to walk the woods, carrying a rifle and be in command of all that lay before me. I needed to own my environment, not be a slave to events out of my control. It had been some time since we had gone camping or I had had a chance to walk the woods. My family is not spontaneous and normally takes a while to "prepare" for any sort of weekend trip, so the thought of taking them along added even more stress. Besides, I really wanted to be by myself to work some things out.

I called my wife and told her what I was feeling and she suggested I pack up, and head up to the Ranch. She and the kids would relax that night and then get ready and meet me Saturday afternoon. I could have Friday night all to myself, and the family would camp together Saturday night. What a wonderful girl!

So I arrived at home, changed clothes and threw the BOB and my shooting bag into the truck and headed for the country. I was feeling better already. I was confident I had everything I needed as we live in hurricane country and the BOB's are always inventoried, packed, and ready.

I lost time because the traffic moving out of the city was heavy, and I had to stop for gas. The Ranch is a few hours away, so by the time I got there it was dark. This was not a concern since we are prepared to operate at night. Even though I had yet to invest in night vision, we often joked that WE OWN THE NIGHT.

I arrived at the Ranch, disconnected the gate security system and parked the truck. It was a warm, beautiful night; and I was absolutely on cloud nine.

I soon encountered my first problem, as my head-mounted flashlight had been packed in such a way that the light had turned on, and the batteries were dead. Using the truck's lights, I found the spare batteries, but could not remove the small cover screw because the screw driver head on my multi-tool was way too big.

Note to self: Make sure you have a tool for every screw on every piece of kit.

I used a lighter, heated the screwdriver and melted the plastic around the screw head until I could get enough grip and removed the screw. I replaced the batteries and promptly dropped the tiny screw on the ground, where it remains to this day. I found the duct tape and could get a partial connection by wrapping the battery cover. I must have looked like an 80's Discotheque with that strobe light on my head.

Note to self: With critical equipment always have a spare.

I put on my load vest without issue. It contained my normal equipment including a couple of spare magazines, dump pouch and rifle maintenance kit. It felt good to put it on again as it had been a while since I had used it. My pistol and hunting knife rounded out the load.

I then proceeded to put on the big backpack. This is a large unit that was custom fitted for me and contained all of the camping gear, food, water and other required items. We are regular campers and its contents were well-tested. It weighs just over 60 pounds fully loaded. I quickly realized I had another problem. Normally, when we camp, we help each other into the packs, and I was now alone. My struggles to get into the pack were probably comical if someone had been watching. What seems like such a simple task was proving to be very difficult. I finally set the pack on the tailgate of the truck and slid into the harness. **It didn't fit.**

I had worn this pack several times. I had worn this load vest several times. I clearly had never worn them both at the SAME TIME. The extra girth created by the load vest and its equipment was interfering with harness of the pack. Normally, this would not be THAT big of a problem except that adjusting all of those buckles, straps and snaps in the dark while a strobe light is flashing was proving to be quite the challenge. I had to become familiar with the pack's harness system, something that had been done for me in the store when I had purchased it and forgotten about since. The truck's headlights bailed me out.

NOTE to self: Know every piece of your gear. Every SINGLE PIECE!

After 15 minutes of trial and error, I was discouraged, tired and above all else – EMBARRASSED. Here was the great outdoorsman, teacher and prophet of preparing, and I couldn't even get a pack on. What a fool.

Finally everything fit, and I began to feel a little better. I grabbed my trusty rifle, verified the safety was on, popped in a magazine and slung it over my shoulder, and dropped directly to my knees in pain. It seems that the extra thickness of the load vest and pack straps interfered with the rifle sling just enough that the barrel hit me right in the privates – HARD.

Of course, the headlamp fails at the same time; and my rifle barrel, supporting my weight, goes deep into the soft soil. After uttering every curse in the known universe and then asking the lord for forgiveness, I manage to get to my feet and walk off the pain.

What a joke. I had been working for over an hour just to get into my gear and had not made it ten feet from the truck. I thought to myself, *"I wonder how many years of teasing I would have to endure if I just throw it all back in the truck and headed home?"* Here was the great warrior, commander of all that surrounds him, limping home with his tail between his legs because he couldn't even mount up and make it to a campsite.

I managed to get the headlamp working by using the backup flashlight on my vest and more tape. *(By this time my pride had made me determined not to use the truck headlights.)*

Note to self: Rubber bands might be a good item to include in your BOB.

My renewed light source allowed me to see a rifle barrel full of dirt and grass. I weigh about 200 pounds and had on another 70 pounds of gear. All that weight had pushed the rifle barrel into the ground about three inches, and I was concerned it was plugged. My maintenance kit at that time did not include a rod, just a pull-through cleaning cable. I didn't want to walk back to the campsite without the rifle. While the boogie man was not a concern, feral hogs were. They are thick in that part of the country and will charge a man if provoked.

So I proceeded to whittle a twig to the right size and put it through the barrel.

Note to self: Find a cleaning rod that will fit in the maintenance kit.

I was finally ready to start the hike back to the campsite.

There is no need to continue this dialog. Before I reached the campsite:

- I was spooked by a horse and fell into a pile of fresh manure.
- I didn't have any towels or soap in my pack.
- My rifle became tangled in my sling and broke a buckle.
- My load vest was so hot, I completely soaked my clothing.
- I not only uttered every curse in the known universe, I created several new ones.

The point being is that I thought I was prepared. My family and I had camped, hiked, and practiced more than any other Preppers I know. I felt like a complete idiot.

Before I tried my solo camping trip again, I made so many trips to sporting goods stores to purchase replacement gear that I lost count. All of the expense and time aside, the damage to my ego was what really hurt.

My experiences that day were a driving force in writing this book. Why did I write a book over something so simple? It is the simple things that will cause failure. Like any other complex activity, you have to master the basics first.

I also thank the good Lord that I learned all of these lessons on a practice run, and not when someone was trying to take my food or harm my family.

Contents

1. The Methodology of Preparing

When it comes to complex objectives, such as the preparing for a defensive role, many have found that a proper methodology helps navigate all of the options, parameters and decisions one is faced with.

Before purchases, plans, practice or even serious thought, establishing a set of rules, tests and steps can help to accomplish any goal or solve any problem. This is really not complex if given a little consideration.

When it comes to any type of preparation activity, here are some example rules and tests that can applied to the process:

i. **Do No Harm** – Do not implement any plan that will <u>harm</u>:
   o The value of my property
   o The lifestyle of my family
   o My moral character
   o My code of life and behavior
   o My position as a law-abiding citizen and patriot

ii. **Dual Purpose** – Any investment in equipment, time, stress or training should serve a dual purpose. This is so that over the long term, frustration, empathy and *buyer's remorse* do not occur.

   Example: Camping gear can be dual purposed for, of all things, CAMPING! This is a recreational activity, something fun and useful. Since we live in Texas, we have to bug-out in case of a hurricane. This is a likely event, so our camping gear is also our Bug-Out Bag (BOB).

iii. **People will be the biggest problem.** In this methodology, people are to be avoided. Plans, equipment and supplies are all derived with an emphasis on AVOIDING PEOPLE.

iv. **You and your family are people, and thus, still the biggest problem.** So much has been written about the mental state of survival that it does not need repeated here. However, anything to be included in the plan should improve the mental state of the group, or at minimum, not degrade it.

v. **When it comes to equipment or skills, look at the military option first.** Many have found that military grade equipment is designed to be used by conscripts with little training under high stress conditions. It is also designed to last for long periods of time in the field under harsh conditions. With weapons, such as the AR15, it is difficult to find a larger stockpile of ammo, spare parts, general knowledge and interchangeable components for any other weapon in the U.S. Some equipment can be significantly less expensive if sourced at Army Surplus stores.

The Military is NOT the best at everything, including gear. Consider Uncle Sam's typical backpack - The regular issue military pack is not nearly as comfortable as a custom fit pack from a quality hiking supplier. I look first at the Military for tactics and equipment, but always see what the private sector provides as well.

vi.   **Everything must work at night.** Half of the time, everyone is going to be in low-light conditions, and this can take some getting used to. Want to have some fun? Ask your children to set up a tent at night. Make sure to film a video for YouTube of that one. *My family is set up to drive, eat, camp and operate weapons at night.* One word of warning – operating at night, in a covert way, is EXPENSIVE. This normally involves Night Vision or Infrared (FLIR) equipment. If the Location enables you to simply use candles without concern for #3 above (people seeing the light), then a large expense can be avoided.

So before adding any piece of equipment, plan or action, follow the methodology:

Will taking this step or creating this item hurt property value? Will it do any harm?

1. Is this equipment something that serves a dual purpose? Will it help in day-to-day life or even be useful in a hurricane (or other common event) plan? Is there a way this item can be engaging or fun for my family?
2. Are other people required to operate or execute? Can my family unit operate this tool or execute this action, or will other people need to be involved? Will this help avoid other people and enable more independence?
3. Will this tool or task burden the family workload? Can the family operate the equipment or execute the task? Will "it" cause additional hardship? Will "it" eliminate hardship?
4. What does the military use or how do they solve "it?" How do the experts in the field do "it?"
5. Can "this" work at night? Can it be "operated" at night?

I hope everyone will perform the same tests or establish similar rules with the contents of this book.

2. Prepper Formal Attire

Dressed to Kill

In a SHTF or TEOTWAWKI life, people will have to become more self-reliant. Many of the services we depend on may no longer be available. One of the responsibilities we may have to assume is our own defense or security. Even today, it is common for people to carry a concealed weapon on their person or in their vehicle for security. Many of us carry a pistol or rifle with a spare clip or two. This is considered enough "firepower" to handle virtually any situation unless we are in a very remote area. The probability of being in a prolonged gunfight is low since law enforcement will eventually respond.

This may not be realistic in a TEOTWAWKI situation. There is a reasonable chance that law enforcement will no longer be available. In addition, the number and ferocity of potential attackers could increase significantly given a desperate population.

No Police + More Bad Guys = TROUBLE

In a post-collapse world, it is reasonable to assume Preppers would be a prime target of opportunity and thus at greater risk than the average citizen. The fact that we will be better fed, equipped and healthier than the typical person may make us an attractive target.

Since you may be solely responsible for your own defense, how you equip yourself deserves some serious thought. I believe it is safe to predict that you will have the following requirements in a post-TEOTWAWKI life:

1. You will be moving around, performing many different activities. Food gathering, trash disposal, scavenging, visiting neighbors, patrolling the house after hearing a late night noise, etc…etc.
2. You will want to have some defensive and survival equipment on your person at all times. You never know when some rogue is going to get between you and your domain or when someone is going to approach when you are outside. You might even get "chased off" or lost while scavenging.
3. While you want to carry at least minimal gear, you will probably need your hands free to garden, field dress, work or simply fill a bucket from a stream.

Everyone has seen pictures of soldiers wearing harnesses and equipment. The equipment looks like dozens of pouches sewn onto a shirt. The military calls this category of gear **"load-bearing equipment,"** and it includes packs, rucks, and other items.

From a certain perspective, soldiers going into a war zone have a lot in common with the typical Prepper:

- They have to plan to stay alive
- They need the equipment and skills to survive
- They may be alone and thus have to carry what they need
- People may be trying to kill them

It has been this way for thousands of years. Militaries have invested a considerable sum researching how a trooper can carry what he needs and still walk, march, run, climb and of course, **fight**.

They use an important rule that we all should follow as well:

The Equipment Train is Pulled by the Mission

The "Mission" or goal for Preppers will change, depending on a variety of circumstances and conditions. It may change day-to-day. Flexibility is the key so that the load can be configured for the day - the "mission." Different equipment would be carried on a short hike than would be required for an extended camp. If hunting, the needs are much different than if going on an extended scavenging journey. Role is also a factor in that a medic carries different equipment than someone planning for a gunfight.

Regardless of the goal, the "freight cars" should all connect together so that they can be "pulled" just like a railway. With a freight train, there are several different types of cars specifically designed to haul a certain type of cargo, such as boxcars, tanker cars, car carriers and others. Load-bearing equipment requires the same type of containers.

Military load-bearing equipment follows the train analogy where there are different types of equipment designed to haul the variety of "stuff" that a person wants to access. What is important is that all of the different types of railroad cars hook together the same way and roll smoothly down the same tracks. Preppers need that same commonality with survival gear.

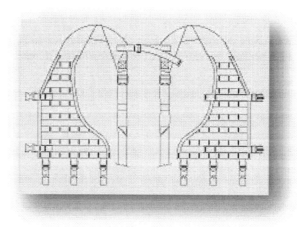

Preppers don't have to worry about the same "load" as a soldier. Warriors, for example, often carry belted ammunition, grenades, radios and other heavy gear that the typical Prepper might like to have – but normally would not tote around.

While there may be differences in equipment, the need to have a flexible, configurable, integrated system to carry equipment is the same. The requirement to have easy access to the load is also similar. No need to reinvent the wheel here; everyone should take advantage of the military's vast experience and research in this area.

Like a train, soldiers compartmentalize their equipment into assorted "freight cars," often referred to as "lines" of gear. Each line is removable, yet connects with others so as to remain stable while moving or running. These lines are often described as:

- First Line – bare essentials to survive the day
- Second Line- what is needed to execute the mission
- Third Line – long term survival needs

Preppers might describe these a little differently:

- First Line – basic stuff to survive
- Second Line – gear I need to hunt, fish, trap, scavenge, garden, defend or patrol
- Third Line – Bug-out Bag

Most Preppers have old gym bags, plastic boxes and hunting vests lying around or currently being used to store gear. All of that is great if one's plan is to remain stationary, but realistically, any plan to remain in a single place is not realistic. Even with a "shelter in place" plan, the concept of being stationary is short-sighted. At minimum, the need to move from one side of the house to the other should be considered. *What if you need easy egress or have to escape?*

So let's begin with the layers or "lines" of equipment a soldier humps and correlate that to what the typical Prepper can take advantage of.

The first important item is the clothing worn under any system.

Most outdoorsmen know the rules about clothing, but I will reiterate the basics just in case you missed it or want to refresh:

1. Cotton[1] is bad, bad, bad. The moisture retention is a problem, so any environment where it can get wet with rain, snow, perspiration or just wading a stream causes your body to react and adjust. Often, with a significant temperature swing, the body cannot adjust. Any inner or outerwear should **not** be cotton. That old pair of blue jeans may be comfy and has great pockets, but can endanger you in some situations.
2. Layers of clothing are always better. This allows for adjustment to temperature changes. Primitive campers have an advantage over the military in this category, with clothing that is more flexible than standard issue BDU (battle dress uniforms.) For example, there are synthetic pants

---

[1] There are materials that are made with cotton combined with other fibers into a "blend." The ability to "wick" heat and moisture away from the body is what is critical.

that have zippers right above the knees and mesh underwear sewn in. They can be unzipped, separated and become shorts for hot weather or swimming/wading. They weigh practically nothing and fold up into a very small pouch. They breathe very well and dry in minutes. Like almost any type of clothing, a variety of colors are available so that blending in with the surroundings of a BOL is an option.

3. No single item is more important than footwear.[2] When on a tight budget, it is recommended to invest here first. It's important to consider that walking while carrying significant, additional weight may become a common activity. Army surplus stores carry used combat boots in excellent condition, and they are not expensive. Make sure to get the type of footwear that is designed for the right environment – like desert boots as compared to jungle boots. Hiking and camping shoes are great, and are often lighter and more comfortable – but more expensive. Whatever the choice, **BREAK THEM IN**.

4. The blouse, or above the waist clothing, will take on more criticality when using load-bearing equipment. Selection of a shirt with a collar or turtleneck is important because straps, slings and other shoulder mounted equipment can rub the neck raw. Pulling up a collar to block the sun from the back of the neck is a bonus.

5. An item to consider is a padded undershirt, sometimes called a "compression" shirt. It has thin "pads" on the shoulders and other places where equipment rests or rubs.

After clothing, the next layer (if body armor is not being used) to be adorned would be the basic load vest or load gear. These come in numerous different configurations, colors and models. Before picking any "system," an introduction to Miss Molly is in order.

MOLLE (*pronounced Molly*) is an acronym for Modular Lightweight Load-carrying Equipment.

For anyone who has ever had to hump a heavy load, MOLLE is a sweetheart of a girl. MOLLE replaced our old girlfriend, ALICE, who was known as All-purpose Lightweight Individual Carry Equipment.

MOLLE is the "hitch" on our equipment train cars. She allows the connection of dozens of different types of pouches, bags, flashlights, tools and containers into a "system."

MOLLE equipment has two basic parts:

- The Base
- The Attachment

---

[2] If you have younger children, you have a problem with footwear. They GROW! Consider stocking up on several sizes of used combat boots (about $20 a pair) just in case. Who knows – if they don't get that big you might barter with the boots later.

The Base item, whether it is a vest, belt, pack or other component, will be manufactured with rows of what appear to be "loops" sewn horizontally to the item every inch.

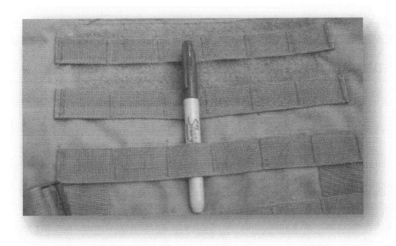

1 - MOLLE Base with Three Rows of "Loops"

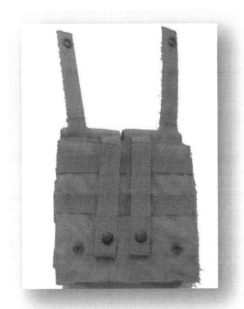

2 - Base Attachment with 2 Straps Extended

The Attachment, whether it is a pouch, holster, container, canteen or other item has a series of vertical straps and snaps.

To connect an attachment, simply <u>weave</u> the straps through the loops on the base and snap to secure. The strips are designed to hold in combat conditions, where running, diving, and hitting the deck are common.

The picture (# 3) below is of a MOLLE Attachment being woven[3] into a Base. Once all of the straps are in place, snap the attachment onto the straps and a secure connection is in place.

---

[3] The technical term for this is PALS, or Pouch Attachment Ladder System – just in case you wanted to know.

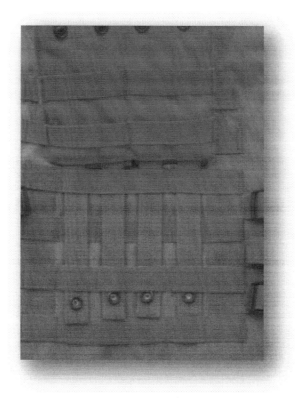

3 - Weaving an Attachment to the Base

MOLLE Attachments come in hundreds of different configurations from different manufacturers. Some flashlight vendors even make the "belt clip" on their product specifically to fit MOLLE. The same applies to many popular holsters and knives as well. Several different types of attachments will be addressed in detail in later sections.

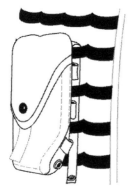

Some people initially run the straps through the loops, out the bottom and snap them together.

THIS IS INCORRECT.

The straps should be **woven** between rows of the MOLLE Base unless the straps will only fit through two rows. This provides stability and lessens the chance of the attachment falling off.

4 - THE WRONG WAY!

5 - MOLLE Attachments of Various Sizes and Types

2.1 The Base

For the average survivalist, there are four relevant types of **Base** Carriers that everyone should become familiar with:

1. Plate Carriers
2. Load Vests
3. Chest Rigs
4. Belts

Each type of base unit has strengths and weaknesses. As the methodology in Chapter 1 suggests, a dual role for any equipment being purchased is desirable. Since MOLLE is available in several different colors from black to coyote brown, any "non-survival" application should be considered as the following sections are analyzed. Hunting, fishing (yes, MOLLE makes a great fishing vest), camping and even weapons training classes are some alternative uses for MOLLE.

6 - MOLLE Load Vest

Plate Carriers look like a vest and are designed to carry body armor "plates," or Kevlar plates, to stop bullets and fragments. While body armor is becoming more common and affordable, most Preppers will probably choose soft sided armor over actual plate armor.

Soft sided armor comes with its own vest, so a Plate Carrier would be unnecessary. The armor plates are "inserted" into compartments sewn on the inside of the vest. Unless the plan is to use plates, avoid having a plate carrier as the internal pouches waste space, add weight, and cause discomfort.

Load Vests are almost identical to Plate Carriers except they don't have the internal pouches. Vests provide the most real estate for attachments. They also tend to have the widest area of support over the shoulders, so the straps don't "dig in" as much. The negative about vests is they are **HOT**. The material used to make MOLLE Base items must be robust to handle quite a bit of weight, and that normally translates into poor venting of body heat[4]. For cold weather areas, vests are recommended. For warmer areas, consider a Chest Rig (below). Both Load Vests and Plate Carriers commonly have internal water bladders (or at least a compartment) built in to accommodate drinking water.

Chest Rigs differ from Vests in that they have straps or suspenders over your shoulders to carry the load. Chest Rigs are normally smaller than vests and open in the back – thus they are cooler to wear. They don't have as much real estate for Attachments and often do not have a snug fit like vests. The equipment may shift around more with a rig, but they are adjustable. Many professionals use Chest Rigs that attach to the belt on their pants in order to stabilize the "up and down" motion when walking or running.

Climbing should be taken into consideration as well. While the typical Prepper is probably not going to be scaling any serious mountains in a post-TEOTWAWKI life, climbing trees, fences and hilly areas may be common. One of the most common mistakes made when selecting MOLLE gear is failure to verify that the arms can be fully extended over the head. The other potentially important position is a prone shooting position.

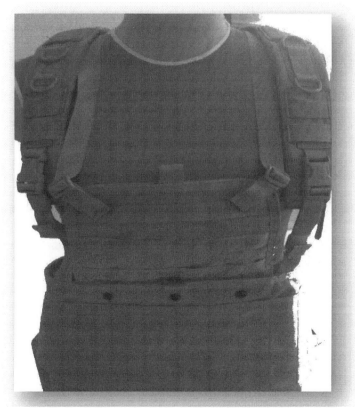

7 - A Common Load Vest with Four Attachments

---

[4] In Iraq, it was common to fill the water bladder with ice if available. This kept the soldier "cool" for a short period.

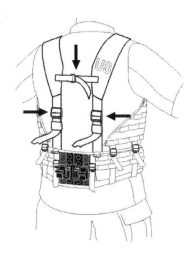

One word of caution about Chest Rigs – Wearing a pack, rifle sling, and chest rig will result in three sets of straps over one shoulder. These can become a major annoyance. When shopping for a Chest Rig, look for the flat, wide straps. Padded straps (*see # 7*) may look more comfortable, but they can cause all kinds of tangles.

Belts are sometimes called "war belts" or "battle belts" and are basically the same concept as a policeman's duty belt – except for the MOLLE ladders. Belts typically have the least amount of real estate of any type of MOLLE base. Some of the larger Chest Rigs are actually a "belt," but have suspenders to help support the weight. Some guys like to wear a Chest Rig and a Belt attached to the bottom of the Rig for support.

8 - MOLLE Chest Rig

8 - Battle Belt

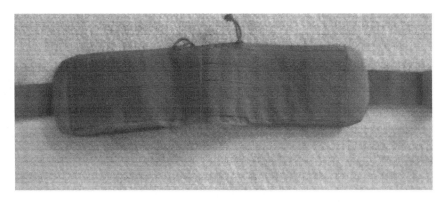

Regardless of what type of base is selected, MOLLE items are not expensive. Army Surplus stores carry older military models (be careful that it is MOLLE and NOT ALICE as they look similar) for as little as $10 per Vest or Carrier. New Base units range from $40 - $300, depending on the quality and configuration.

It is highly recommended to take an afternoon and go try on several different models. If possible, try to find a store that won't mind the customer bringing in a rifle and sling to make sure everything works well together. However, before any purchase is made, there are several more decisions to make about attachments and gear. It would not be prudent to purchase a base unit until all of the items you plan to carry are identified.

2.2 Attachments

MOLLE Attachments come in so many different shapes, sizes, colors and configurations some manufacturers have entire catalogs devoted to them. What is important is that they ALL will fit on a MOLLE base unit. The connection is standard, just like a hitch on a railway car.

One of the most common examples of a MOLLE attachment is a magazine pouch. Soldiers carry lots of magazines when fighting. It is not unusual for a modern day trooper to have 8 or more on his/her person. Even with magazine pouches, options such as bungee secured, closed flap snap, close flap Velcro and others are available.

Most Army Surplus stores or "Duty" clothing outlets carry dozens of different types of MOLLE Attachments for just about every possible configuration. Here are a few of the more common ones:

- Medical kit
- Dump pouch – used to store empty magazines or other discarded items you don't want to leave on the ground. (empty magazines and power bar wrappers)
- Holsters for your secondary (pistol)
- Flare pouches
- Grenade pouches (smoke grenades for most of us)
- Weapons maintenance kit and spares
- Night Vision
- Radio or Walkie-Talkie

MOLLE Wallets are even available. In addition, it is possible to clip flashlights, pens, glow sticks, knives and even 12 gauge shotgun shells to MOLLE.

9 - MOLLE with Various Attachments

A few notes about MOLLE Attachments:

- They are rarely waterproof. While most will keep the contents relatively dry even in a strong rain, critical items should be sealed in a zip-lock bag if there is a chance they will be submerged or if they are required to withstand downpours. Specialized waterproof attachments are also available, but uncommon.

- MOLLE attachments can be used for all kinds of smaller items, such as gardening tools, mechanical tools and cell phone holsters. While thinking about a TEOTWAWKI existence, don't just think weapons, combat supplies and survival gear. Think of it as a method to carry items, having quick access to them, while keeping both hands free.

3. Prepper MOLLE (1st Line Gear)

Now that all of the basics have been covered, the next logical step is to determine what is required to be carried by Miss Molly. This is really not a difficult task, as one of MOLLE's greatest advantages is its flexibility, so changes to our configuration can occur at any time. Let's take two example "missions" to see how MOLLE would work with each.

The "on guard" or "patrolling" Prepper would want to carry the following inventory:

- Rifle Magazines (3)
- Pistol Clips (2)
- Medical Kit (Blow out Bag)
- Rifle Maintenance Kit (both to clean and maintain)
- Radio
- Night Vision
- Binoculars (if not using high power optics)
- Map (maybe)
- Compass (maybe)
- Flashlight (in addition to a weapons light)
- Rain Gear
- Knife
- Water (enough for a thirsty day)
- Food (just a little)
- A dump pouch

This would be our equal to a soldier's "First Line Gear" - enough to keep a Prepper in the fight, or to live for the day.

10 – Our patrolling prepper items ready to go into a pack or ruck.

If the patrolling Prepper's inventory were thrown into any old bag, it would look something like the picture above when dumped out to find an item.

Placing all of this equipment[5] onto a good MOLLE rig, like pictured below in #12, would allow everything to be within reach. This would also be more comfortable than a bag thrown over the shoulder.

---

[5] I highly recommend Smoke Grenades as part of any Prepper kit. These are not shown.

11 - MOLLE Patrol Layout

A. Radio
B. Secondary (Pistol) with extra clip
C. Magazine for Rifle
D. Rifle maintenance kit and Night Vision Device
E. Medical Kit (blow out bag)
F. Dump pouch with rain coat, extra magazine, Jell-O and power bars
G. Knife
H. Flashlight

With this setup, there are three rifle magazines totaling 84[6] rounds. Not enough for a long term gunfight, but plenty to break contact and hightail it back to the BOL. If the trip involved going into an area where trouble were expected, one could easily configure MOLLE to have 8, 10 or even 15 magazines (if the weight were not an issue).

The map and compass (not shown) are in a zipper lining on the rig. A back mounted water bladder provides hydration, and good optics on a rifle eliminates the need for binoculars or additional optics.

---

[6] I don't put 30 rounds in most AR magazines because it increases the potential for jamming. Only loading 28 seems to work the best. The number 84 equals one on the vest, one in the dump pouch and one in the rifle.

While this may sound like a super heavy load, in reality, it is not. Most people who don a MOLLE vest for the first time are surprised at how much weight they can carry comfortably.

The Food Gathering MOLLE would require a list similar to the one below:

- Extra Magazines (1)
- Extra Clips (1)
- Medical Kit (Blow out Bag)
- Rifle Maintenance Kit (both to clean and maintain)
- Radio
- Binoculars (if not using high power optics)
- Map
- Compass
- Flashlight (in addition to a weapons' light)
- Knife
- Water (enough for a thirsty day)
- Food (just a little)
- Plastic Bags

The above list can be carried in just five pouches. The possibilities are practically endless.

Some MOLLE Attachments are quite large. The picture below *(# 13)* shows a common MOLLE "Dump Pouch" with a standard tissue box inside and plenty of room left over. While on the topic, a Dump Pouch functions exactly how it is named – it is a personal "dump" or where any garbage is stashed. Empty magazines and anything else that can't be discarded on the ground can be placed into the dump pouch. It is similar to a common trash bag hanging on the back of a car seat.

12- MOLLE Dump Pouch with Tissue Box Inside

All of those small, pesky items can be kept in a pouch and attached as needed for the day. If the day's activity is hunting, then take the field dressings' knives (in the pouch) and connect them to the vest.

If the plan is to be gone for a while, hook up an additional pouch with extra food. After returning, just unhook the "extras," and sit them by the door.

If a group is going out, there may be no need to take two medical kits. Unhook one, and add something else that might be required. This allows the balancing of loads among members of the group.

3.1 2nd Line Gear

Backpacks with MOLLE Bases can also be useful. Again, being able to configure the "load" according to the goals (Mission) is what is so vital to Preppers. A transfer of various attachments from a chest rig to a pack can be accomplished in short order.

13 - Backpack with MOLLE Base

As most campers and hikers know, a problem with any **size** backpack is – **its SIZE**. It seems they are always too large or too small for the next activity. MOLLE solves this problem in that extra pouches can quickly be attached to the outside of the pack.

Hikers commonly go into a wilderness area with a heavy load, set up camp and then take one or more "day trips." Afterwards, they return to the primary camp. With a MOLLE rig, simply attach what is needed for the day trip and leave the rest behind.

3.2 3rd Line Gear

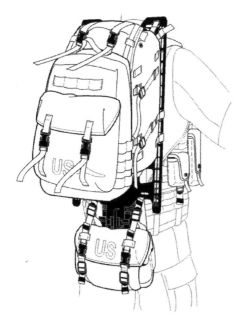

One of the best setups for a Bug-out Bag is a large backpack. While MOLLE "backpacks" are available of equal size, most people find that hikers have the advantage in comfort and weight- bearing harnesses over any military models.

There are several good sources to pre-shop for large backpacks on the internet.

A few notes on selection:

1. A quality pack is not cheap. They can range from $150 - $600 and should allow for a lot of adjustment.
2. Know what is required (equipment-wise) to be carried before shopping for a pack. At minimum have a general idea of the weight of the load. It is common to see a person bring their BOB contents (no weapons or ammo) in a plastic bag right into the camping store. Don't be shy and call ahead if concerned over the store's policies.
3. A quality store will have sand bags to test the pack. These are placed into the pack after it is fitted in order to simulate a load. The clerk should then adjust the pack to your body and ask you to move around with the load. Don't accept any other method for this level of investment. A poorly fitting pack can cause all kinds of issues and pain later.
4. Try on several different models. The highest price does not always equal the best pack. Load it up with weight and walk around the store for a while.
5. Make sure you wear any TEOTWAWKI clothing when going shopping. This is especially true of footwear. Don't be shy. If it is a quality store, they will expect this.

14 - Large Backpack as a Bug-out Bag

*My BOB has more equipment in it than I want to carry day-to-day. I do not normally carry a shovel, 20 pounds of water, tent and sleeping bag with me on day trips. The method I have found that works best is to keep my 2nd Line pack **inside** of the BOB. I keep food, medical kit, magazines, extra food, stove, and other smaller items in individual MOLLE pouches as well.*

15 - BOB Contents

A. Mess Kit and large metal cup with pot holder and flint & steel inside
B. Silverware
C. Water purifier
D. Hoo-hahs (baby wipes) and assortment of plastic bags
E. Shovel and spare tent stakes
F. Rope
G. Sleeping Bag
H. Spare clothes and socks
I. Spices, medicine, 2 lighters and spare batteries
K. Stove (WWII German Army Model) and fuel
L. Duct Tape and Fishing Line
M. Rain Poncho (make sure it will fit over the pack)
N. Hatchet and Glow sticks
O. Food
P. Microfiber towels (2)
Q. Soap, Insect repellant and Sun Screen

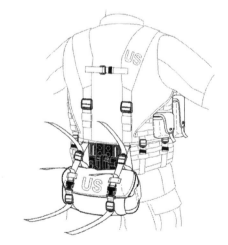

Any of the above items will fit in MOLLE Attachments, with E, I, K already being packed that way.

Depending on the plan for the day (the "mission"), a selection is made and connected. MOLLE allows anyone to have a complete modular system that is inexpensive, flexible and allows heavy loads to be carried comfortably.

3.3 Working with MOLLE

A cardinal rule among Military professionals is:

Train how you will Fight

For Preppers, this takes on a slightly different meaning than for the typical soldier. Most Preppers are older and have regular daily activates like jobs, children, hobbies or other duties. They cannot engage in maneuvers, exercises and drills like a full-time Soldier or Marine.

However, there are several types of "training" that can be performed by the average person. These will serve to prepare everyone should a critical need suddenly arise. The knowledge and experience of how to properly use MOLLE and a BOB should not be left to the last minute as it may be too late.

The first order of business, after acquiring any gear, is to balance the loads. Since MOLLE is a shoulder-based load system, it would be prudent to pack everything, strap on a rifle and walk around the house. *While the wife and kids may think you are a little "touched," the teasing now will be less painful than sore shoulders and blisters later.* The goal is to achieve balance. Make sure that the gear is balanced left to right or side to side. *You also can extract revenge by making everyone test their load as well.*

The second task is to verify everything can be reached that is mounted on MOLLE. Can the spare clips be pulled out? Can the secondary (pistol) be drawn without tangling it up in something? Do the spare rifle magazines come out ready to be inserted (rather than flipped around) into the rifle?

The third task is to make sure everything is comfortable moving into a shooting position with a rifle. Does it get hung up on a pouch? Does it feel good on the shoulder and allow a proper cheek weld?

While checking the rifle, make **SURE** that a "transition" to the pistol can be executed well. There is no need to be Wild West Gunslinger quick – smooth is fast under stress. Can the spare clips for the pistol be easily reached?

The last item to verify is that walking is comfortable with everything on. *I have been known to walk around the house doing chores with my rig on – just to make sure nothing rubs me the wrong way.*

Once everything is comfortable and secure, the next step is creating ways to "train" with MOLLE.

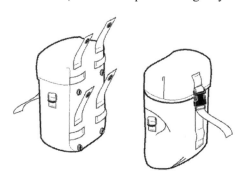

4. Training with MOLLE

The best way to train with MOLLE is to have access to private land that can be used to hunt or walk for extended periods. Climbing fences, jumping creeks, ascending hills and wandering through valleys will quickly indicate how well MOLLE is working. Of course, the more physically fit someone is, the easier this will be.

If taking Miss MOLLE on a date to somewhere private is not an option, then the next best thing is called a "weight vest." These are available at almost any sporting goods store and are used by athletes to perform endurance training. They have 12-20 small, sewn in pouches that contain removable sand bags. The weight can be adjusted by removing or adding the little sand bags and thus gradually increase it over time. These are flat, non-military looking vests and can be covered up with a sweatshirt or loose jacket. Simply go for a walk around the neighborhood. No one will know that a secret training program to become a MOLLE equipped operator is in progress. The exercise is probably good for everyone regardless.

I also believe in loading up all of my gear and going up and down the stairs a few times. Even an active person will be surprised at the effort this takes.

For the average Prepper, there is no need to be able to pass a Military fitness test while wearing the gear. The most important capability is to be able to walk reasonable distances with the equipment.

The MOLLE chest rig above (#12) weighs less than 12 pounds fully loaded with weapon and everything. Many businessmen commonly carry a computer bag, cell phone, wallet, car keys and bottle of water. All of this would weigh just 2 pounds less. They often walk through airports, parking garages and to meetings carrying almost identical weight. The average lady's purse can't be far behind in the weight category. If an umbrella or raincoat is added, the weight is almost equal.

For the second and third line gear, the absolute best way to "train" is to camp and hike with it on. There is no need to wear the "military" looking MOLLE vest and frighten all the hikers and park rangers. This is another reason why it may be prudent to select a non-Military backpack. Privatized gear can be worn anywhere without issue. While carrying a rifle is out of the question (unless on private land), any option to become familiar with the weight of the equipment is a positive.

If a bicycle is part of the plan for TEOTWAWKI transportation, ride it with the pack on. Make sure it does not stress back muscles or interfere with balance, braking or other actions. The same applies to a horse or any other method of transportation.

For elderly folks, or those who have a physical limitation, a common "golf bag caddy" may be an option. These little hand pulled "carts" are typically robust and designed to carry a lot of weight. They are very inexpensive, and a good size backpack would fit perfectly on one.

4.1 Personality Conflicts with MOLLE

It is possible to simply not "get along" well with MOLLE. With everything connected, loaded and practiced, she can remain uncomfortable and disputes are common. Don't give up! There are several options available to mend the relationship.

A common disagreement with MOLLE is the rifle magazine sticking out from the body of the rifle and becoming entangled with the MOLLE pouches. An AR15's 30 round "mags" take up a lot of space and extend a few inches below the rifle. They can get hung up on gear, bang legs and cause issues. One idea is to carry a 10 round magazine (much shorter) in the rifle when not expecting trouble. It is smaller and less intrusive. These can also be carried on the vest or chest rig to reduce weight.

Most MOLLE rigs are very adjustable and having someone else pull straps, tighten buckles and generally custom-fit MOLLE can help.

There are under-MOLLE tops called "Compression Shirts" that have padding where the typical MOLLE weight rests and rubs. These shirts can make a tremendous difference in the comfort level of the gear.

Finally, weight can be reduced in several ways. If the rifle is comfortable, mount a flashlight on the rifle rather than on the MOLLE Base. The same can be done with night vision or NVD.

Look at every single component and see if a lighter piece of equipment is available. Many times, a weight-saving unit that will perform the same function is an option. *I recently discovered an ultra-lightweight rifle cleaning kit that reduced weight over the model I had used before.*

Again, the Military professionals have a saying:

Ounces = Pounds and Pounds = Pain

Even if a different equipment option only saves a few ounces, it will all add up. Always be on the lookout for lighter gear even if MOLLE is already comfortable. If nothing else, carrying more food or water could be important if additional weight capacity is available.

Chapter 10 focuses on weight reduction and its impact.

4.2 A Girl with a Bad Reputation

Unfortunately, MOLLE is a girl with a bad image. It seems that every radical, anarchist, zealot and revolutionary likes to make a video holding an AR15 and wearing a MOLLE vest. These extremists post home movies on the internet and spout whatever nonsense is on their minds. One video even showed a gentleman who was holding a **BB gun** that was made to look like an AR15.

This has propagated a stigma that anyone, other than the military or police, wearing a MOLLE rig belongs to this radical group of people. Perhaps being radical and selecting good equipment can be mutually exclusive?

Of course, wearing a MOLLE rig to the mall, even without the pistol or magazines, would no doubt cause people to point and whisper. Who could blame them? Wearing a computer bag to a rifle training class would probably cause a more overt reaction than whispering.

MOLLE should not be avoided because of this stigma. It can be part of an integrated system of defense that may be critical in the future.

In a post-TEOTWAWKI life, we may not enjoy the convenience of accessibility by today's standards, so we may have to carry what we need with us. If the police are no longer protecting us, we may carry more clips. If ambulance service is no longer an option, we may carry a medical kit on our person.

MOLLE may save your life one day.

4.3 Taking Good Care of MOLLE

MOLLE components are actually very robust and designed to withstand extended abuse in the field and during battle. With that being said, MOLLE will occasionally need a bath. Perspiration, mud, grime, gun oil and other environmental exposures can make MOLLE a dirty, smelly girl.

Pre-TEOTWAWKI care is as easy as washing MOLLE Base units like a car, with regular laundry soap and a scrub brush. Rinse well and hang to dry.

MOLLE components can be placed in the household dish washer, although allowing them to go through the heat drying cycle is probably not wise. That can make some of the pouches "tight."

Post-TEOTWAWKI, simply soak everything in a bucket and hand dry.

One tip on cleaning MOLLE gear is to "lube" the snaps on the attachments with a little gun grease or petroleum jelly after washing.

Another tip concerns mag pouches. By design, you want your rifle magazines to be like baby bear's soup – just right. They should be "tight" enough to keep the mag secure, yet free enough so that you can pull out the mag quickly and freely. When washing or cleaning your gear, I recommend drying them with a mag inside the pouch to retain the shape and size of the pouch. There should be no issue with drying[7] these pouches with a Mag inside of them.

---

[7] The Army does not recommend drying MOLLE gear in the sun as it can induce rot. I do not recommend drying MOLLE gear in a clothes dryer because it can damage gear and dryer. MOLLE doesn't need to be washed often anyway, so I use the sun for drying.

4.4 A Working Relationship and Tattoos

Regardless of how a kit is carried, the carrier needs to be able to access it. This means placing the items needed the most frequently or with the most urgency, where they can be easily reached. Seldom used items can be mounted to the back of the Base.

A variety of circumstances will affect the location of MOLLE pouches and how they are prioritized. If in a rural area, where no one has been "seen" for weeks, it would be reasonable to be comfortable with the magazine in the rifle and not so concerned about reaching any backup quickly.

If picking berries, slinging a rifle over your back, rather than having it constantly banging into your legs would be reasonable as well.

Soldiers give a lot of consideration to the placement of MOLLE pouches. They want their spare magazines right in front where they can reach them quickly. Unit Medics may want their IFAK (Improved First Aid Kit) in a specific position. Who can blame them? In reality, for the average Prepper, everything mounted on MOLLE load gear is going to be accessible in a reasonable amount of time. Unless in an environment where there is constant fighting, the difference in time to access a front-mounted pouch versus one on the side is not going to make that much difference.

Comfort will probably be more important than one half second access times. How the load is balanced or how well it "rides" while moving around is what will be more important day-to-day.

It is also wise to give MOLLE some tattoos – or mark the outside of the pouches with permanent ink symbols so that anyone can find specific equipment quickly. If the person carrying the medical kit is hurt, another person may need to find it quickly. The medical kit should have a few red crosses marked on the outside. If equipped with multiple calibers of rifles, mark the various MOLLE pouches with the caliber they are made for.

Soldiers have Velcro patches that identify their blood type on the outside of their rigs. This lets a Medic know quickly without searching for "dog tags" or other identification. In a post-SHTF world, blood transfusions will probably be rare, so it is difficult to see a lot of value for this, but it can't hurt. If anyone's blood type is unknown, a "typing kit" can be purchased for under $20 or anyone can donate blood, and the donor will be typed in that process.

4.5 Military MOLLE

If you served and were issued a specific MOLLE attachment or base that you would like to order, the list below is the DOD reference numbers (MSN) for all standard issue MOLLE equipment.

- MOLLE, Rifleman, Complete pack Set   8465-01-459-6572
- MOLLE, SAW Gunner, Component Set   8465-01-459-6580
- MOLLE, Grenadier, Component Set   8465-01-459-6582
- MOLLE, Pistolman Component Set   8465-01-459-6584
- MOLLE, Combat Medic Component Set   8465-01-459-6585
- MOLLE, Waistbelt, Molded, Small   8465-01-465-2109
- MOLLE, Waistbelt, Molded, Medium   8465-01-465-2110
- MOLLE, Waistbelt, Molded, Large   8465-01-465-2111
- MOLLE, Bladder, Hydration   8465-01-465-2096
- MOLLE, Pouch, Grenade, Hand   8465-01-465-2093
- MOLLE, Pouch, Magazine, M16A2, Double (30 rounds)
        8465-01-465-2092
- MOLLE, Pack, Patrol   8465-01-465-2088
- MOLLE, Belt, Utility   8465-01-465-2082
- MOLLE, Adapter, ALICE Clip   8465-01-465-2062
- MOLLE, Pouch, Magazine, M16A2, Single (30 rounds)   8465-01-465-2079
- MOLLE, Pouch, Utility   8465-01-465-2070
- MOLLE, Set, Buckles   8465-01-465-2080
- MOLLE, Pack, Butt   8465-01-465-2058
- MOLLE, Pouch, Radio   8465-01-465-2057
- MOLLE, Straps, Lashing   8465-01-465-2095
- MOLLE, Vest, Load Bearing (LBV)   8465-01-465-2056
- MOLLE, Pack, Frame   8465-01-465-2158
- MOLLE, Carrier, Sleep System   8465-01-465-2124
- MOLLE, Carrier, Hydration   8465-01-465-2131
- MOLLE, Pouch, Sustainment   8465-01-465-2152
- MOLLE, Straps, Shoulders, Frame 8465-01-465-2133
- MOLLE, Pouch, 6 Magazines, Bandoleer, M16A2   8465-01-465-2144
- MOLLE, System, Hydration   8465-01-465-2154
- MOLLE, Pack, Main   8465-01-465-2289
- MOLLE, Pouch, 9mm Magazine (single)   8465-01-465-2155
- MOLLE, Pouch, 200 Round SAW Gunner   8465-01-465-2263
- MOLLE, Adapter, K-Bar   8465-01-465-2272
- MOLLE, 40mm High Pyrotechnic Double   8465-01-465-4445
- MOLLE, 40mm High Explosive Double   8465-01-465-4417
- MOLLE, 40mm High Explosive Single   8465-01-465-4416

5. MOLLE and Camouflage

Military Snipers are famous for their use of camouflage and being able to avoid detection. One of the most common forms of camouflage is called a Ghillie Suit.

16 - Example of a Ghillie Suit

Anyone can purchase dedicated Ghillie Suits at most hunting supply stores or through the internet. These typically come in two varieties with either the "foliage" pre-attached or as an empty suit of webbing that the owner uses local foliage to weave into the suit.

Having a dedicated Ghillie Suit is a good idea if there are plans to hunt, scout, or scavenge. It is not an expensive item. Make sure to consider changes of season (and thus the color of surrounding vegetation) if a dedicated Ghillie is part of any plan.

MOLLE can be used as a "poor mans" Ghillie Suit if necessary. All of those rows of loops used to mount attachments can also be used to hold small stems of local branches, twigs and clumps of grass.

For desert environments, take cardboard and spray paint it the color of surrounding rocks and sand. Cut the cardboard into shapes and leave strips just wide enough to stuff into the MOLLE loops. While imitating the exact shape of a rock is not feasible, it is important to remember that affective camouflage simply breaks up the outline of shapes the human brain is trained to recognize. It is also possible to take strips of cardboard and cover them with thin layers of glue. Just sprinkle sand on the wet glue and let it dry. The same method can be used with strips of cloth.

5.1 Taking MOLLE to a Costume Ball

There is a worthy debate among Preppers over using a "Passive" profile versus an "Active" profile in a post-TEOTWAWKI life. While the *HOLDING* series of books addresses this debate for a BOL, the same arguments can be made for one's personal appearance as well.

A Passive profile would invoke an appearance that projects, "I am unworthy of robbing or harassment. I am poor, staving and have nothing of value."

An Active profile would assert, "I am a badass. If you even come near me I will kick your sorry butt. There are easier targets, so MOVE ON."

In reality, the situation and environment will dictate which works best for any individual:

- If in an urban area, perhaps where organized gangs are in control, the passive option may be best.
- If in a rural area where trouble is seldom encountered, the active profile may work well.

Another consideration is an individual's capability to fight. With the active profile, one is brandishing weapons and demonstrating skills. If the person has a lack of fighting expertise, their equipment may be taken away from them and then used against them. TEOTWAWKI will probably not be a good place to bluff.

Some might conclude that using MOLLE or similar methods to carry equipment would contradict the principle of "Hiding in Plain Sight," but this is not necessarily true. If asked, practically any Law Enforcement Officer will verify that they are trained to look at pockets, belt lines and bulges under jackets. They may watch the hands and eyes, but they scan for hidden objects first when there is the potential of confrontation. The point being that no matter how equipment is carried, it will most likely be visible unless precautions are taken. If this reasoning is followed through, it means that a passive profile would only work if all equipment were left behind since it can't be hidden. This is a false assumption.

The Military learned quickly in Iraq that it was not beyond the "insurgents" to dress up like females,[8] with loose fitting "dresses" that contained several pounds of explosives under them.

In a TEOTWAWKI situation, dressing up like a female may not be such a good idea. In the USA, where females are "treated" completely differently than Middle Eastern cultures, looking like a lady may attract predators rather than allow anonymous movements. Even today, many women shop, choose parking spots and progress through life with the potential of sexual assault on their minds. In there any reason to expect this unfortunate reality would improve after TEOTWAWKI?

---

[8] While I cannot verify the accuracy, I have been told that the Army actually advised soldiers to "look at their toes – men have hairy toes" due to this method of disguise. One has to wonder if the insurgents thought about shaving their feet.

What may be an affective disguise is to appear as a bum - down and out, hard up and not worth any assault. This would be difficult, but not impossible, while carrying a lot of MOLLE equipment and even a rifle.

Countless professionals prefer a rifle with a folding stock. Many of the newer generation of Battle Rifles, such as the FN SCAR and Remington ACR have folding stocks to reduce the overall length of the weapon. This is not a new concept as airborne units discovered this advantage over 50 years ago.

The "folding" or "paratrooper" stock was common in WWII with M1 Carbines. Paratroopers, by design of their mission, have to carry more equipment with them than "normal" troops with support behind them. The Soviets came to the same conclusion as many models of the AK family have folding stocks.

A shorter weapon means it is easier to hide under a jacket or overcoat. It will also be less likely to become hung up in gear and straps.

There are several options with weapons, including Bull Pup designed rifles, Short Barrel Rifles (SBR) and many, many others. Depending on the situation, just carrying a pistol may be enough.

If any part of the "plan" involves being able to "Hide in Plain Sight," a few considerations should be analyzed:

1. Acquire (garage sales are great sources) large, oversized clothing as part of the plan. These should be items to cover your MOLLE gear and perhaps a rifle.
2. A blanket or shawl can be used as cover. Depending on the area and weather conditions, this could be a good choice.
3. Fast access to any weapon is a must. With a blanket or shawl, this is easy. With a jacket, overcoat or extra-large shirt this can be slower.
4. A poncho can be used if rain is common or expected. Access to a weapon underneath would be more difficult.

The amount of time and money invested to create a disguise ultimately depends on each specific situation and environment. An urban or suburban BOL would probably justify a detailed, practiced disguise. Halloween is always interesting for people who trust in this method.

Appearing as someone who is down and out, or a "homeless person" as they are called these days, may be worth the time. Some homeless people are obviously just that – homeless. Tangled hair, dirty clothes, hollow stares, unshaven and mismatched wardrobes are typical "signs."

It might be worthwhile to secure a shopping cart and fill it full of stuff to push around as well.

The variations on TEOTWAWKI life can include all kinds of bizarre predictions and are probably unworthy of consideration in any plan. What the average Prepper should consider is identification of the other "humans" in the area and the visible signs of the "haves" and the "have nots."

6. Weapons Maintenance Kit

As stated above, in a TEOTWAWKI existence everyone will have to perform a wider variety of tasks than in current times. Today, if a weapon malfunctions or breaks while shooting, either a spare is used or the shooter heads home to repair it. In a world where each person is responsible for his or her own defense, the luxury of "just" going home to fix it may not be an option.

Soldiers in a warzone typically have access to a unit armorer (gunsmith) once back from the field. But while they are on patrol or a mission, they are on their own. Both Soldier and Prepper share the need for self-reliance.

I interviewed several recent combat veterans as well as researched an extensive amount of material to compile the contents of my "Fix it" kit. In addition, I used the lessons I have learned from over 30 years of active shooting.

The first step in determining what should be in any maintenance kit is dependent upon the type of weapon(s) that will be used. Every major weapons platform has several differences:

- What tools (if any) are required to field strip the weapon?
- What tools (if any) are required to completely strip the weapon?
- What tools are required to clear the typical failure or "jam?"
- What typically breaks?
- What typically wears out?
- What special tools (if any) are required to clean the weapon?

Answers to these questions, for both the primary (rifle) and secondary (pistol) guns should be obtained. If the plan includes any additional pieces, such as a shotgun, they should be researched as well.

Many people choose military-grade weapons for several reasons, one of which is they are designed to be cleaned and cleared by conscript armies of young, inexperienced troops. It is reasonable assume if "those kids" can survive with the weapon, then it should be easy for anyone.

Most shooters can effectively "field strip" their guns. There are a few folks out there who have not taken the time to increase their skill set to include this expertise. This proficiency should be gained NOW while there is access to teaching videos and manuals on the internet or bookstore. In some cases a special tool or method is required; if so, make sure it is in the kit.

There is an ongoing, worthy debate over the need to completely strip any weapon in the field. In today's world, it doesn't make sense carry that capability (and weight) around all the time. In a SHTF world, one may have to bug-out or egress from the BOL in a hurry. Being able to maintain your weapon in the field may be critical. For a common type of blaster, the AR15 platform, nothing special is required to break it down. Everyone should be sure of their choice of weapon.

I shoot over 20,000 rounds a year, so I know how my weapons fail. I have experienced every type of FTF (Failure to Feed), jam, double feed, and stovepipe you can think of. It is a bad feeling when you pull the trigger and hear that dreaded "click." I always advise people who can't shoot as often to purchase the cheapest, lowest quality ammunition they can find. Shoot it with an unoiled, dirty weapon. You will learn a lot about your gun and failures.

Often, a common household flathead screwdriver combined with a cleaning rod will fix most jams on most platforms. As an example, if a lot of rounds are fired through any weapon, the shooter will eventually pull the trigger and hear a small "pop" and then a failure to feed or extract (on an autoloader). This, according to most experts, is the most dangerous failure there is. What has happened is that the round had a primer, but no powder. The bullet left the brass, but only progressed a few inches into the barrel. If the shooter were to manually load another round and pull the trigger, he will be slamming the 2nd round into the 1st, inside of the barrel – and that can't be good. This type of failure can be fixed with a common cleaning rod by just ramming the stuck bullet out of the barrel.

If the resources or time to fire thousands of rounds through the weapon are unavailable, another option is to inquire at the local gunsmith. Do not seek assistance with this problem at a gun store as their business is selling weapons and may they may not be candid. Another great resource is the internet. There are hundreds of gun forums and blogs, many of which address specific platforms or brands of weapons. Again, if the choice is to run a "Joe Nobody Arms Mini-14," don't rely on the official Joe Nobody Arms website and their forum – they may remove forum posts that are negative about their products. A better choice would be to investigate venues where there is less control over posts and content by manufacturers.

While researching platforms (remember these rules apply to every weapon in use), the following information should be noted as well:

- What typically breaks?
- What typically wears out?

As a source concerning breakage and wear, gunsmiths just can't be beat. Another excellent source for military-grade weapons is the manufacturer's maintenance schedule. Even Russian AK47's have published maintenance schedules that indicate which parts should be replaced or inspected after n number of rounds. For example, one of the most common items to "wear out" on the AR15 platform is the actual firing pin. After 6,000 rounds, the military inspects them. These are a low cost, small item, so to carry a spare is not a big expense even if one has never failed before.

Other than failures and wear, the other major function any kit needs to address is cleaning. In reality, with enough lube, most weapons will function for hundreds, if not thousands of rounds without cleaning. Some "experts" believe that concerns over cleaning in the TEOTWAWKI existence are unnecessary as there won't be enough ammunition or usage to "worry about it."

Others disagree strongly, but not for the reasons one might think. Post-TEOTWAWKI life is likely to be VERY stressful and difficult to maintain a positive mental state. The capability to perform common, everyday actions like shaving, brushing your teeth or cleaning a weapon are going to be important to all of us. The need to shave and clean a weapon may not be critical, but some might feel better if they do. The cost, space and weight of equipment required to clean any weapon is low, so why not have it? The average gun owner should have 99% of these items anyway.

6.1 The MOLLE Maintenance Kit - Example

The example post-TEOTWAWKI kit really has nothing in it that would not be used by a typical shooter on a weekly basis. It is small, light and therefore easily accessible when needed.

Figure 17 - MOLLE Maintenance Kit (D)

In the preceding picture, item **D** is a Maintenance Kit. As shown, it is not very large and weighs less than 1lb. It is a non-waterproof, zipper top MOLLE pouch. The location of the pouch was selected for a couple of different reasons:

1. It is the right "length" for the sections of barrel cleaning rod (that screw together) and other tools that are included in the kit.
2. It is relatively "flat," so it does not interfere with weapons or with going prone (on the belly) to shoot.

Some people would disagree with having the least used pouch right in the middle of the "work area," or the area directly in front of the shooter. Their logic being that the owner would be better served by having magazines or other Attachments where they can be reached quickly. *While the placement of MOLLE pouches is covered in section 44, I have tried several different configurations, and this one works best for me.*

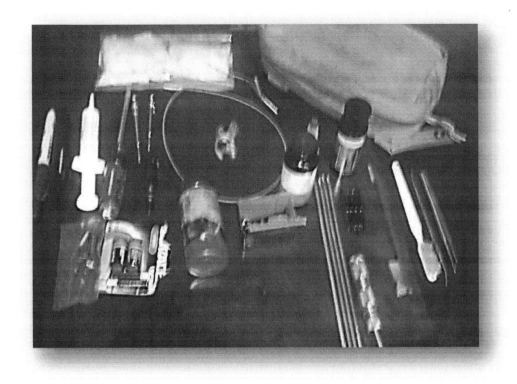

18 - Example Maintenance Kit

In Picture 16 above, an example Maintenance Kit is shown. It contains:

- Cleaning Patches
- Cleaning Cable
- Grease
- Optics cleaning "pen"
- Writing Pen
- Screwdriver
- Spare Firing Pens (two calibers)
- Spare Bolt (AR15)
- Ear Protection (spares)
- Solvent
- Lube
- Brushes
- Small screwdriver set
- Dental Tools (for cleaning mostly)
- Barrel rod (pieces screw together) and base
- Every size hex wrench required by scope mounts and weapons in small box
- Plastic bottle with bore brushes and tips
- 1911 barrel wrench (you can do it by hand, but this is easier)

- Spare batteries required by optics and gun light
- A Spares kit (every spring in my weapon)

Everyone's content will be different depending on what types of weapon(s) are selected. Springs, as an example, may or may not be a concern. A shotgun would perhaps require different items. The same applies to various pistols. *I have never experienced a single "break" on a 1911 pistol after tens of thousands of rounds, so I don't carry any spares.*

Pistols are often small enough and inexpensive (as compared to rifles) that duplicate units serve as spares kits.

It is also advisable that everyone verifies they have the right cleaning brushes and tips for all of the different types of weapons.

7. The Defensive Medical Kit

There are hundreds of sources available for TEOTWAWKI medical needs and supplies. For the defensive role, it is necessary to address the portable, personal kit. More specifically, it is a kit designed to treat gunshot wounds or other injuries resulting from a fight. Long ago, when researching the best components for a medical kit, two very knowledgeable sources were consulted:

- Military, Combat experienced Medics (Corpsman)
- An ER Nurse

For a person who is not a medical professional, the first instinct may be to go purchase a typical, off-the-shelf kit and put it into a MOLLE pouch and be done. This would probably be a waste in that most of the available kits are lacking in some critical items and have other pieces that would never be used.

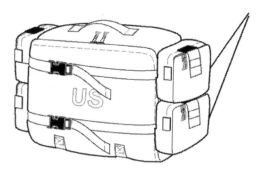

It is also surprising to discover the variety of opinions among Army Medics. There are significant differences between various units and what their medical specialists want their soldiers to carry in their kits.

One of the most frustrating exercises involves **pain control**. If someone is "hit," controlling their pain to avoid shock and allow immediate care is a basic of first aid. What they don't tell you in classes is what to stock in a kit to accomplish this. Military and EMT professionals have fast-acting pain control devices that contain narcotics. The typical Prepper is not going to have access to these tightly controlled substances. Many Preppers plan to stock leftover prescription pain killers, but these are normally administered orally and can take 15-20 minutes to become effective.

Imagine a gunfight with looters, and someone on your team is hit. They may be screaming in agony, writhing or jerking on the ground. The first priority is to stop the bleeding, but they are out of control with pain. This would make the application of any sort of treatment very difficult. Focus, which is hard enough with an injured comrade or loved one, will be even more difficult if they are suffering. *What are you going to do? Pull out your little packet of aspirin[9] and say, "Here – take these?"*

Many medical professionals, when questioned about the above situation, will say that everyone reacts differently to different types of gunshot wounds. Some soldiers (both ours and theirs) have been reported

---

[9] Some medical sources cite that Aspirin increases bleeding.

to continue on with the fight for several minutes without even knowing how badly they were injured. Other wounds are immediately debilitating and cause extreme reactions. Unfortunately, a good, fast acting solution to pain control remains an open issue.

Everyone should determine the priorities of their group, and keep them simple when it comes to a portable medical kit. As an example (and probably a very good one), the first priority of the kit should be:

STOP THE BLEEDING

Anything short of minor scrapes, cuts or abrasions is probably beyond the untrained Prepper. While carrying items required to clean a minor wound is prudent, 90% of any defensive kit could be devoted to stopping a major hemorrhage. If this can accomplished, it gives the injured party a chance until either help can arrive or they can be moved to a better equipped location – like a BOL.

The example kit is labeled as **E** in picture #18. It is small, lightweight and non-intrusive. The contents are shown below:

19 – Example Contents of MOLLE Medical Kit

The specific types of bandages, dressings and other items are really not relevant as so many brands, sizes and types exist they are easy to source and very inexpensive. Maintain an assortment of bandages.

Some items that are worthy of note are as follows:

Tweezers – If people are shooting at each other, there will be broken glass, splintered wood, plaster, bricks, stucco and any other numbers of small piercing objects around. Wood splinters or glass shards in the body can become infected at worst, and be an annoyance at best. Tweezers are invaluable for retrieving these little invaders.

EMT Shears – At the very top of any kit should be the shears. If someone gets hit, chances are it will be in an area that is covered with clothing. Worse yet, it may be under multiple layers of MOLLE Base, rifle slings, belts and pouches. Being able to cut away all of that to get to the wound is critical. While a hunting knife may get the job done, the chances of harming the victim with the knife are greater than if using shears.

Tampons – One of the cheapest, best wound packing materials around. They are sterile and small and the perfect shape to stuff into an entry wound. According to the TV commercials, they absorb a lot of liquid as well.

Wrapping – Some good advice, provided by an experienced Army medic, is to carry more tape and "wrapping" bandages than a normal first aid kit. These can be important when applying multiple "Layers" of dressings. Large amounts of tape or wrapping can be required. In summary, you can never have too much tape.

Packing – When equipping a kit for a gunshot wound, it is common for these types of injuries to have an entry and an exit wound. The entry wound is often very small, while the exit can be quite large with severe tissue damage. Having more "packing," or larger gauze bandages is recommended to prepare for this situation.

While 100 medical experts could look at any kit and add an additional 100 items, a comfort level should be achieved with the contents and the knowledge to use them well. Additionally, a good balance of weight, size and cost should be your goal. Always keep in perspective the likelihood of ever having to use the kit. It is easy to "overdo it" and purchase various items that require more knowledge than the average person possesses. No one should carry equipment they don't have the expertise to use.

8. Head Case

Most Preppers don't put much thought into hats and headgear. Like most clothing, there are many choices ranging from the common baseball hat to a military helmet.

Most people quickly rule out a helmet due to its weight. While the concept of being able to mount night vision to a flip mount is attractive, the weight and discomfort are difficult to justify. While they do provide added protection against some gunshots and shrapnel, most Preppers decide against adding one to their kit. If the decision is made to go with a helmet, they can be purchased at army surplus for around $100.

Many people wear baseball hats in their normal life, but there are a few issues with them in defensive roles:

1. The bill of the hat hits often "bumps" into rifle optics. *This seems to affect some shooters while others commonly wear a baseball cap.*
2. They do nothing to protect the back of the neck from the sun.
3. Probably the most critical item is **they do not keep rain from flowing down the back of the neck.**

A popular solution is the common "bush" hat that was originally made famous by Special Forces in Vietnam.

20 - Typical Bush Hat

Even within the "Bushy" category, there are several options, including MOLLE attachments (*not shown in 21*) around the brim.

Another reason why they are so popular is that a small Mosquito net can be stored in the top without discomfort. It can even attach to the inside of some models if necessary. A "bug net" is highly recommended to cover the head and neck areas.

Regardless of what type of headgear is selected, it should meet a few requirements for TEOTWAWKI:

1. It should keep the rain off of the head and stop it from running inside of the poncho or other rain gear.
2. It should keep the sun off of the back of the neck.
3. Any "storage space" or attachment points are a plus.
4. The area's weather conditions should also be considered. A climate that experiences very cold weather requires a hat that would be uncomfortable in warmer areas.
5. Most important of all – **it should allow a weapon to be shouldered and aimed without interference or discomfort.**

You have literally hundreds of options for hats and headgear. Motorcycle helmets, paintball gear, hockey masks and other sports-related equipment can all be used.

8.1 Mug Shots

Like headgear, most Preppers don't pay much attention to any sort of mask or balaclava. Unless you live in cold climates, covering your face is unusual, and in some places even illegal.

21 - Common Balaclava

Covering the face should be considered, even if you reside in a temperate climate. There are several reasons for this:

1. When people are shooting at each other, especially within structures, there is flying glass, plaster, wood splinters and other high velocity junk in the air. Covering the nose, mouth and skin can make a difference.

2. Even the most southern regions of the U.S.A. get cold from time-to-time. While they may not experience artic weather, having at least basic protection on all exposed skin can help in a survival situation.
3. Having a face covering may be advantageous at certain times. Aside from illegal activities, if someone is in a confrontation or negotiation with looters, they may not want the others to be able to see their face.
4. A mask looks serious, if not nasty. Humans are programed to read other people's facial expressions, and taking that away has several implications.

There are so many options for face masks; any attempt to reference all of them would be futile. Masks can be functional items as well, such as cold weather models that are quite effective.

Some manufacturers make evil-looking patterns on their on their face masks that may intimidate others. Masks are available in skull patterns, zombies and even aliens. The choices are practically endless.

Face masks are very inexpensive, with some military surplus models costing less than $3.00.

A few items to consider before purchasing a face mask:

1. **Weight** – Again, Ounces = pounds and pounds = pain.
2. **Eyewear** - The unit should allow for eyewear, even if the wearer doesn't require glasses. Glasses should always be worn when fighting due to flying debris.
3. **Weather** – Specifically, the conditions at the BOL. If it gets cold, this can be a great addition to any kit. If it gets hot, make sure it is a light weight version.
4. **Color** – Most masks are far more comfortable than face paint. Make sure the color you select helps with any personal camouflage.

8.2 Gloves

Aside from the obvious benefits of cold weather protection, those who have spent any time working with their hands already understand the value of gloves.[10] In a defensive role, they take on a slightly different role; however, many professionals do not like wearing gloves during combat.

To reiterate, during a gunfight there are all kinds of nasty debris flying around; and in a post-TEOTWAWKI world, even the smallest cut or splinter can cause serious issues if antibiotics are not available. *Even if you have a good supply, do you want to use up your stock on something silly that a simple pair of gloves could have prevented?*

Gloves in a defensive role also address the problem of hot weapons. Rifle barrels become VERY hot with just a few rounds put through them. After 20 rapid rounds through an AR15, the barrel will peel skin right off of a hand.

---

[10] Home improvement stores and auto parts supply stores offer pretty good gloves. Contractors and mechanics both have a similar need to soldiers regarding hand protection. These gloves are inexpensive as well.

Like most articles of clothing, there are hundreds of choices for gloves. One option would be dedicated "fighting" gloves with exposed fingers so as to manipulate weapons controls and other small items.

Some soldiers like to have very thin finger covering but lots of padding on the knuckles and back of the gloves.

Whatever choice is made, be certain that both the primary (rifle) and secondary (pistol) can be operated with the gloves. For thick, padded cold weather gloves, verify that AT LEAST the trigger finger fits well.

8.3 Rain Gear

Being able to stay dry and warm will probably take on a whole new meaning in a post-TEOTWAWKI life because even a minor cold could turn into something more life-threatening without today's common medications.

Hunting or scavenging trips may become critical, and delaying these outings due to weather might be out of the question. *Fair weather looters?*

For rain gear, it is difficult to find a better solution than a common poncho.

The primary reason why is because a poncho can cover someone wearing MOLLE, a rifle, a pistol and even a pack. The requirement is to keep equipment and clothing as dry as possible, and a poncho can accomplish this.

There are several different materials and designs on the market. Some guidelines for making a purchase are as follows:

1. Make sure the poncho will cover the largest pack.
2. Verify that it can be put on over all equipment while that equipment is being worn.
3. Find the right combination of "breathable," yet lightweight and compact.
4. The material should be rugged and able to withstand abuse.

A poncho can also be used as emergency shelter and some older military models were engineered to be one half of a "pup" tent.

There are other alternatives if a poncho will not work. Another potential source would be clothing designed for sailors or golfers.

9. Other Body Parts

Many people use **kneepads**. A defensive role may require many actions that are painful to the knees. Going prone quickly, shooting behind cover, and dropping to a knee for a braced firing position are all examples where knees can suffer abuse and pain. It is common when carrying a heavy load to "take a knee" to rest. Many people choose to wear a single kneepad, as they normally take the same knee, unless the type of cover requires a different stance. Kneepads are **not** comfortable, so it makes sense to wear only one. Kneepads can be adjusted to ride at the ankle if walking long distances without concern for having to go prone. If the pad is at the top of the boot or ankle, it is hardly noticeable.

Most hardware stores carry quality kneepads. The same can be said of home improvement stores as construction workers use them all the time. There seems to be very little difference between dedicated military models and construction models except the price is much higher for the military brands.

Ear protection is strongly recommended. Models that fit "in-the-ear" can let regular sound be heard (like talking or shouted communication) but will block the majority of rifle discharge. Shooting in an enclosed area, like a home, can permanently damage the ear. The potential of injury aside, communication among team members during a gunfight is critical. It would be silly to lose communication at a critical moment because everyone had lost their hearing. Soldiers have helmet linings and the ear flap to protect hearing somewhat. They also commonly have a radio earpiece in at least one ear. The combination of a radio earpiece and a single $1.50 earplug can be effective. Other models amplify sounds, which may be advantageous and can cost $300 or more. Be aware of battery requirements.

It cannot be stressed enough to have **eye protection**. While some people believe "shooting glasses" are for protection against exploding guns, in reality, they are for flying debris and smoke. A popular option is referred to as "wrap-around" glasses. The Army issues goggles, but these can have fogging issues, especially with tight sealing models. Many people have to wear prescription glasses to read, so eye protection takes on a whole new list of requirements.

It is also common to wear sunglasses. The combination of safety glasses, sun glasses and prescription glasses can be difficult to find in a single set of lenses. Yet changing glasses right in the middle of being ambushed can also be difficult. There are solutions, commonly marketed for sports such as motocross and mountain climbing, and are worth the investment.

22 - Great Eyewear!

The above example is capable of:

- Prescription lenses
- Transition lenses (they get dark in the sunlight)
- Adjustable seal or fit (magnetic insert shown in #23)
- Safety lenses
- Solid frames that will withstand abuse

These glasses were discovered by an optometrist when looking for sports based eyewear. This specific model was designed for motocross riders.

If prescription lenses are not required, there are several over the counter choices available. Most gun stores or duty supply stores will have options ranging from $30 - $500 depending on budget and needs.

10. Losing Weight

If most scenarios about post-TEOTWAWKI life are realistic, our lives will require more movement on foot than what is common today. Many believe that we will spend more time walking with a considerable load than we do now. One Prepper commented that when he purchased a new truck, the experience changed his mind. As he was cleaning out the old truck and moving everything to the new one, he was shocked at how much "crap" he hauled around every day. He listed coins in the console, flashlight in the glove box, SHTF kit under the seat, toolbox in the bed and much more. He estimated 100 pounds of CD's, maps, a knife, weapon, two clips and who knows what all else.

My friend's experience got me to thinking: In reality, we won't carry "more crap" with us. Post-collapse, we will actually carry less because we won't have a big V8 engine to help us haul that load.

What will become critical is choosing very carefully what is carried and to think like primitive campers think – EVERY OUNCE IS CRITICAL.

A serious primitive camper weighs every single piece of equipment before making a decision. To reiterate:

OUNCES = POUNDS and POUNDS = PAIN

I was in a high end camping store and picked up a combination spoon, fork and knife tool for eating. It was marked $98.00. This struck me as odd since I know I can purchase an almost identical set at a sporting goods store for around $6.00. About then the clerk came over and said, "Those are really something aren't they, we just got those in and they are on my wish list."

It ends up that I was holding a set made of TITANIUM. It was all the rage because it weighed .56 OUNCE less than a quality aluminum set. The store claimed not to be able to keep them in stock.

Now I like to eat over the campfire as much as the next guy, but really?

There are some steps that everyone can take regarding equipment that will save weight and are reasonably priced. Some of these solutions are less expensive than heavier gear.

A favorite piece of camping gear is a German Infantry, WWII ESBIT cooking stove. A few companies still produce the exact same model today. It is the size of a deck of cards and works wonderfully to cook or make coffee in the morning when the campfire is out. The unit costs about $5.00, plus a large number of "fuel cells" is an additional $5.00. It weighs about 7 ounces and with 10 days' worth of fuel, that weight doubles. This is **CONSIDERABLY** less weight and cost than a liquid fuel powered camp stove. Several people believe it also works better than a volcano stove.

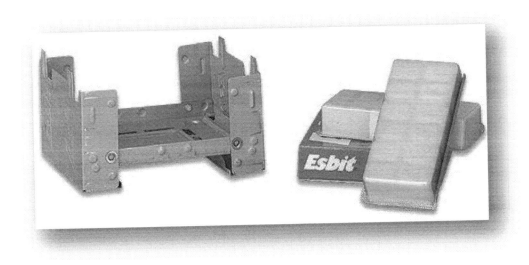

23 - German Camping Stove

Another significant weight savings can be in the form of sleeping bags. While the typical BOB may not include such an item, it may be critical in the future when electric heat is no longer available and wood smoke is a bad idea.[11]

A common sleeping bag, rated at 30 degrees is a good example. The weight ranges between 15 ounces all the way up to 4.6 pounds. That is a significant difference, yet the cost is similar regardless of the weight.

Most Preppers, even if campers, don't think about weight that much. They typically focus on comfort because they can load everything up in the car/truck and head off to the campground. For a TEOTWAWKI life, there might now be a car. You might be carrying all of the equipment on your back.

Tents are another component worthy of weight consideration. The weight range of tents is similar to sleeping bags.

Normally with camping gear, lower weight means higher cost but this is not always the case.

Depending on the BOL area, a hammock can save weight when compared to a tent and air mattress. If you camp often in the desert, trees are rare so there is nothing to hang the hammock from. If the location has a significant number of trees, a hammock would make sense. Modern camping hammocks are really comfortable and are a lightweight combination of tent, mattress and rain cover. Sleeping above the ground has several advantages, including comfort.

---

[11] If the "bad guys" are in the area, wood smoke will draw them to your location.

24 - Typical Camping Hammock with Rain Covers

In a wooded area, it is much "safer" and mentally comforting to sleep above the forest floor, regardless of how secure your tent is. Any experienced camper in the south has encountered fire ants, spiders and other ground crawlers inside of the tent. While a hammock is not perfect, it should be a option for any BOB.

Almost every single item in the kit should be evaluated for weight reduction.

Here are some additional examples:

Rifle Magazines – The composite magazines are just a little lighter than traditional metal mags. While the difference is just a few ounces each, this can add up when carrying several of them. Most serious shooters have been using "plastic" mags for years now. They are less expensive and most shooters agree that they hold up just as well as the traditional metal mags.

Rifle Barrels – Unless you are a long range shooter, the difference between an 18 inch rifle barrel and a 14.7 inch barrel will make little difference in accuracy. The difference in weight can be significant.

Rifle Stocks – While there is nothing like a beautiful, well-crafted wooded rifle stock, they are heavy. Would a composite stock reduce weight?

Ammunition – There is always a debate over how much ammunition to carry. A fully loaded AR15 or AK47 magazine weighs over a pound. Do you really need to carry 4, 6, or 8 fully loaded magazines in a SHTF role?

Multi-tools – Many Preppers love their multi-tools, and there is a strong argument for having one on your person at all times. Evaluate the real usefulness of the larger models as they can weigh over a pound. Skeletonized models are much lighter, and if the can opener is already in the kit as a separate item, weight can be reduced even further.

Flashlights – There is little argument over the value of flashlights. Modern LED flashlights are typically lighter and have longer battery life than older models and their "D" batteries. A light, mounted on a weapon, is common and can be configured with "quick mounts" so they can be used in multiple roles. Head-mounted flashlights weigh very little and while they are not as bright as most handheld models, the light is "focused" on the work area and can be quite effective.

Everyone should manage the weight of their equipment. It is no different than any other part of planning. No one knows when they are going to have to "get out right now," and carry their life on their back.

One method of managing weight and loads is to make a list of all equipment in the assorted configurations that may be used. An example follows:

Item	Weight	Notes
Rifle	7.8	With optics, sling and other accessories
Pistol	2.8	loaded
Magazine	1.2	each
Clip	.55	each
Maintenance Kit	1.4	
Medical Kit	1.3	
MOLLE Vest	1.1	
Etc......		
TOTAL	xxxx	

Then consider how much each "category" of gear adds to the total weight:

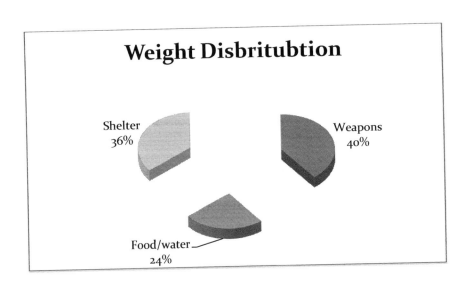

Using this type of analysis gives you a different perspective as to what will be carried and why. If the post-TEOTWAWKI area is a highly populated urban area, then more emphasis on weapons and firepower may be prudent.

If the BOL is rural, then perhaps carrying more food/water is the right plan.

11. Weapons

Choosing a weapon for survival can be a complex process. Most weapons are dedicated to a specific use, such as hunting, fighting, training or target shooting. Weapons (guns) are like automobiles or practically anything else – they are a compromise. In the case of weapons, the compromises are between weight, power, reliability, cost, availability of ammo and all sorts of other factors.

So what is the perfect weapon for survival? **There is no perfect weapon for survival or any other use.** The choice depends on skill level, budget and projected needs. If in a remote area, the logical choice may be a rifle that is focused more on hunting than on security.

If in an urban area, then a weapon designed for anti-personnel usage, like an AK or similar may be a good choice.

Any rifle is a machine, and like all machines, they can break or fail. There are a couple of "old sayings" that should be taken seriously when it comes to weapons:

"**Buy nice or buy twice**" is really true. For the most part, you get what you pay for in a weapon. There are too many manufacturers out there in competition for everyone's money for rip-offs to be common. Will a $1,000 rifle shoot better or last longer than a $2,000 dollar rifle of a similar platform? Not likely. This rule holds true until you start getting into the exotic big game or hunting rifles. Some of these "works of art" go for tens of thousands of dollars and are worth it to their specialized market. *I would not invest in one of these types of rifles for a defense weapon, long range or medium range.*

"**One is none – Two is one**" is another old adage that really rings true. Even the highest quality, well-maintained weapons can jam or break. What is intended by this wisdom is that you need a backup weapon. Most professional soldiers refer to it as a "secondary," and that is normally a pistol. I apply the 1=0, 2=1 rule differently as a Prepper in that I am not sure my local gunsmith will be around to fix my broken weapons, so I have two of all of my weapons for spare parts as well as extras of critical parts in my kit.

While our focus with *TEOTWAWKI Tuxedo* is personal clothing and gear, there are also options for weapon's accessories that directly impact our choice of MOLLE base and attachments as well as our wardrobe in general.

11.1 Personal Optics

Most anyone who spends time in the field knows the value of magnification. This can be binoculars, rifle scopes, range finders and any other number of devices that increase the capability to see at distance. In a survival situation, having this capability may be critical.

As discussed previously, weight is an important factor. There may be a need to be as light and mobile as possible while still maintaining reasonable security. For this purpose, having both a rifle scope and binoculars adds additional weight that perhaps can be eliminated.

Like any technical topic, there are a few key terms and axioms that will help novices understand the world of optics and make solid decisions where defensive equipment is acquired.

BUIS (Back Up Iron Sights) - These are the original[12] post and fork sights that we all grew up with as kids on our BB guns. For over 300 years, iron sights were state of the art. Now, you will notice, they have the name "Back Up." This is because the newer technologies have been proven to be faster on target and more accurate under pressure.

Red Dot – A Red Dot optic is a laser beam that is projected onto a small, clear glass mounted on the weapon. Red dots should not be confused with holographic sights, nor should they be compared with aiming lasers.

When you look through the sight, you simply put the "dot" on the target and squeeze the trigger. Red dot sights are typically inexpensive, with some bargain models going for $30 or less. Be careful, because most of the inexpensive models are not water or fog proof and the battery life tends to be very short.

Most SERIOUS shooters or professionals choose a holographic sight, which operates under the same basic principle, but normally is more robust, has a longer battery life and the most important of all – much less parallax. You will notice in the picture above that the "dot" is off to the side, or off center of the glass. This is called parallax and can cause a missed shot. Holographic sights eliminate a large amount of parallax.

Both of these devices have been proven to reduce target acquisition times.

I can run a shooting course with multiple targets over 20% faster with a holographic sight than traditional BUIS.

---

[12] Professionals don't trust optics much. Batteries can fail; glass gets shattered and other battlefield damage can occur. A real pro learns to use the BUIS first, and this is good advice for the Prepper as well.

In addition, you can keep both eyes open on most models. This increases your field of view and allows you to identify peripheral threats faster.

Holographic Weapons Sights – are similar to Red Dots, but the image seen when looking through them is generated by a holographic device rather than a straight laser beam.

The image on the left shows a typical holographic image looking through the optic. The soldier on the right (showing very bad shooting form) is looking through a Trijicon ACOG optic.

Several beginning Preppers have asked me, "Why don't soldiers use as much magnification as possible? Wouldn't it be better to always zoom in as close as possible?"

The answer to this is no, it is not better and the reason why is target acquisition and the speed of acquisition. A very high magnification rifle scope makes it difficult to find a target close to you, and the typical gunfight is within 200 meters.

For sniping, a high magnification scope is a great help and is commonly used; but for targets inside of 200 meters, it is the speed that you can acquire and fire that counts.

Rifle Scopes come in about as many varieties as actual rifles and pistols. Again, buy nice or buy twice. I think every gun guy in the world has pondered if the higher priced optics are "worth it," especially when the stores are full of much lower cost units. My personal experience is that any rifle scope that costs less than $500 is suspect. Any rifle scope that costs above $3,000 is suspect. The differences between lower cost scopes and the higher priced models are:

Light Transmission – A good quality scope will allow you to see better as light fades.

Hold of Zero – Poor quality scopes will not hold the cross-hairs at zero while mounted on a rifle with heavier recoil. You shoot the rifle a few times and start noticing that you are suddenly missing your targets.

Quality of housing – A good quality scope can be used as a hammer to drive a nail. While this may sound a little silly, if you ever drop your rifle down the side of a cliff and find that the scope is still intact and holds zero, you will think your investment was wise.

Adjustments – A higher quality scope will have more finite adjustments.

A VERY important note to make about any optic or scope that is intended for a fighting gun – don't skimp on the mounting system! A fighting weapon will take more abuse than any hunting weapon and requires a quality, proven mounting system.

So how do you combine a long range rifle scope, which can replace our binoculars, with a short range holographic weapons sight? The following sections will address several options.

11.2 Offset Mounts

An Offset Mount allows for both a large magnification rifle scope and a Holographic Red Dot to be mounted on a rifle at the same time. As shown below, a small red dot is attached to the rifle scope with a mount. This does not harm a high quality scope.

25 - Rifle with Offset Mount

This option allows for a very high powered rifle scope for long distance observation AND shooting, as well as a close in, fast acquisition optic. The small holographic Red Dot weighs just a few ounces and is very effective.

It should be noted that a rifle scope does not provide nearly the field of view as a good pair of binoculars. While it is common to have much more magnification with a modern scope, you will not see nearly as much ground as with a dedicated set of binoculars.

11.3 Combined Optics

Some manufacturers make combination optics that provides both short range acquisition as well as long range magnification. These devices normally do not provide as much magnification as binoculars. While they are normally in the 4x to 6x range, they can provide enough "zoom" to be effective in the field. The picture below shows an ACOG type optic with a holographic sight mounted on top of the scope body.

26 - Trijicon ACOG with Red Dot

11.4 Adjustable Optics

While rifle scopes with adjustable magnification have been around for years, it was unusual to find a model with 1x as its lowest setting. Most hunting or sniping scopes began their magnification at 3x or 5x. This meant that you were already "zoomed" at the lowest setting and thus would have difficulty finding a target close to you.

In the last few years, rifle sights with adjustable magnification beginning at 1x have become common. The model below, from ELCAN is even equipped with a throw lever that quickly takes you from 1x to 4x and back.

27 - Adjustable Optic ELCAN Specter-DR

Any of these options can provide you with a weight savings and still perform well both at long and short ranges.

11.5 Accessories

Accessories (sometimes referred to as furniture) are all of the nice little items you attach or use with your weapon. A sling is an example of an accessory.

Accessories are typically a matter of personal preference and thousands of choices are available. Some of the most common accessories are:

- Slings
- Weapon's Lights
- Rails
- Stocks
- Lasers
- Pods
- Bi-Pods

- Multi-magazine devices

Of all of the accessories, I believe a **sling** is the most important for a defensive weapon. A good, comfortable sling is critical because you will hopefully be carrying the weapon more than shooting it. Slings are categorized by the number of points where they attach to the weapon. Single point, two point and three point slings are the only ones I know of. By far, the most popular is the two point sling.

When you are trying on a sling, make sure you can transition the weapon around to your back. If you are out working in the garden, but feel the need for security, then you are not going to want to hang onto the gun with one hand or have it swinging around your waist and knees. *My personal favorite is the Magpul MS2.*

11.6 Other Equipment

11.6.1   Night Vision

There is a lot of equipment you can purchase to improve your defensive capabilities. Probably the biggest "game changer" I have ever spent money on is Night Vision.

A Night Vision Device or NVD is rated in "Generations," with Gen1, 2, 3 or 4 being currently available. The price and capability increases with the generation number. Think of each generation as a new, improved version.

In addition to the generation of the device, you also need to verify that it is "gated," which means it can withstand bright lights, like the muzzle flash of a weapon, without damage.

NVDs come in several different configurations. You can purchase dedicated weapons sights, goggles and monocles. I have found that the monocles are the most useful in that you can mount them on an AR15 in front of your normal optics (if you purchase the right kind of optics), as well as use them stand-alone.

Some people like to mount NVD on their rifles, while others like a "head mount" or "helmet mount" system.

In addition, you will need to configure your MOLLE load bearing equipment to handle the weight and storage of your NVD.

The typical device is not heavy, but NVD Goggles can be bulky. Any type of head mount will also be a bulky storage problem for MOLLE.

A Generation 3 NVD is so effective you can drive, safely, at night without headlights. Hunting at night is practically the same as in full daylight, and that could be important in a post-event environment. NVD **will not** see through smoke or fog. You need Infrared for that capability.

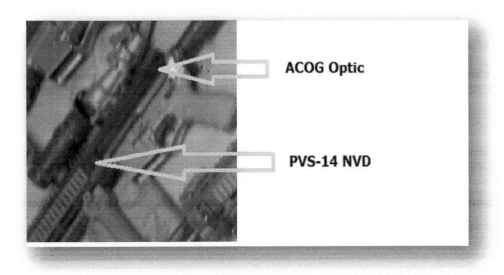

28 - Author's rifle with NVD mounted in front of ACOG.

Unless your foe has NVD, you will own the night. On average, one third of our time on this earth is in low or no light conditions.

As of this writing, a quality Gen-3 Monocle, such as a PVS-14, is about $2900. That is a lot of cash, but again, I can't think of a single item you can purchase for the same money that will improve your capability as much as NVD.

In the last few years, Forward Looking Infrared (**FLIR**) devices have become available to the general public. These units are extremely expensive, ranging from $6,000 to over $25,000. FLIR devices give the added advantage of being able to see through smoke and some amounts of fog. Personally, I can't justify the expense for my intended purposes. I keep an eye on the prices as they continue to decline. When FLIR technology approaches the price of existing Light Gathering NVD, then I will probably consider a purchase, but not before then.

NOTE- NVDs are battery powered. Most take standard sizes, such as AA, so a rechargeable is a valid option.

11.6.2   Body Armor

Body Armor is rated in "levels," such as Level-3 or Level-4.

Level-3 armor is rated to stop all handgun rounds and most rifle rounds fired from a distance. The rating system on Body Armor is very complex because it has to be able to withstand multiple hits in a wide variety of temperatures. For our purposes, we probably won't be fighting in artic conditions.

Level- 4 armor is basically for the Military and the situations they are exposed to. While you may end up in a gunfight, chances are you will not end up being shelled or expect your armor to withstand the effects of missile strikes.

For our purposes, the type of Body Armor is an important consideration because it should work with our MOLLE system and other equipment. Body Armor comes in two basic types:

1. Soft-sided or self-contained armor comes with its own vest and the plates are "built in" or non-removable. This type of armor is normally rated less than Level-4. It is also less expensive.
2. Plate Armor is a series of small "plates" that are inserted into some sort of vest or "carrier" as discussed in *Section 2.1* on Bases. Plate Armor is normally heavier, more expensive and "thicker" than Soft-sided Armor.

Wearing body armor is like having three additional layers of clothing under your MOLLE gear. It can impact the fit of your packs, shooting position and mobility.

If you are thinking of equipping yourself with armor, you should make sure that your MOLLE equipment, and everything else, is adjustable. The typical AR15 rifle stock is adjustable as are normal MOLLE vests and chest rigs. Make sure everything else will fit "over the top" of the armor.

Made in the USA
Lexington, KY
25 May 2012